If you were a

FRACTION

by Trisha Speed Shaskan

illustrated by Francesca Carabelli

PICTURE WINDOW BOOKS
Minneapolis, Minnesota

fraction—one or more equal parts of a whole

Editor: Christianne Jones
Designers: Nathan Gassman and Hilary Wacholz
Page Production: Melissa Kes
The illustrations in this book were created with acrylics.

Picture Window Books
151 Good Counsel Drive
P.O. Box 669
Mankato, MN 56002-0669
877-845-8392
www.picturewindowbooks.com

Printed in the United States of America.

All books published by Picture Window Books
are manufactured with paper containing at least
10 percent post-consumer waste.

Library of Congress Cataloging-in-Publication Data
Shaskan, Trisha Speed, 1973-
If you were a fraction / by Trisha Speed Shaskan ;
illustrated by Francesca Carabelli.
p. cm. — (Math fun)
Includes index.
ISBN 978-1-4048-4790-3 (library binding)
ISBN 978-1-4048-4791-0 (paperback)
1. Fractions—Juvenile literature. I. Carabelli, Francesca, ill.
II. Title.
QA117.S52 2009
513.2'6—dc22   2008006456

Special thanks to our adviser:
Stuart Farm, M.Ed., Mathematics Lecturer
University of North Dakota

If you were a fraction ...

... you would always be a part of something.

You could be one wedge of an apple, two pieces of pie, three wedges of a pear, or four slices of pizza.

If you were a fraction, you would be one or more equal parts of a whole.

The hungry hippo eats a fraction of every pizza on the buffet table. He takes one-half of the vegetarian pizza, one-eighth of the sausage pizza, and one-fourth of the cheese pizza.

If you were a fraction, you could be divided into three equal parts. You would be thirds.

Jenny juggles three red balls. One ball falls. Jenny has dropped one-third of the balls.

Joey juggles three green balls. Two balls fall. Joey has dropped two-thirds of the balls.

If you were a fraction, you could be divided into two equal parts. You would be halves.

The zany zebra's flag is one-half white and one-half black. The loopy leopard's flag is one-half yellow and one-half black.

The proud peacock's flag is one-half green and one-half purple.

1/2

1/2

If you were a fraction, you could be divided into four equal parts. You would be fourths.

One window has four equal parts, or panes.
If one pane is broken, one-fourth of the window
is broken.

If three panes are broken, three-fourths of the window is broken.

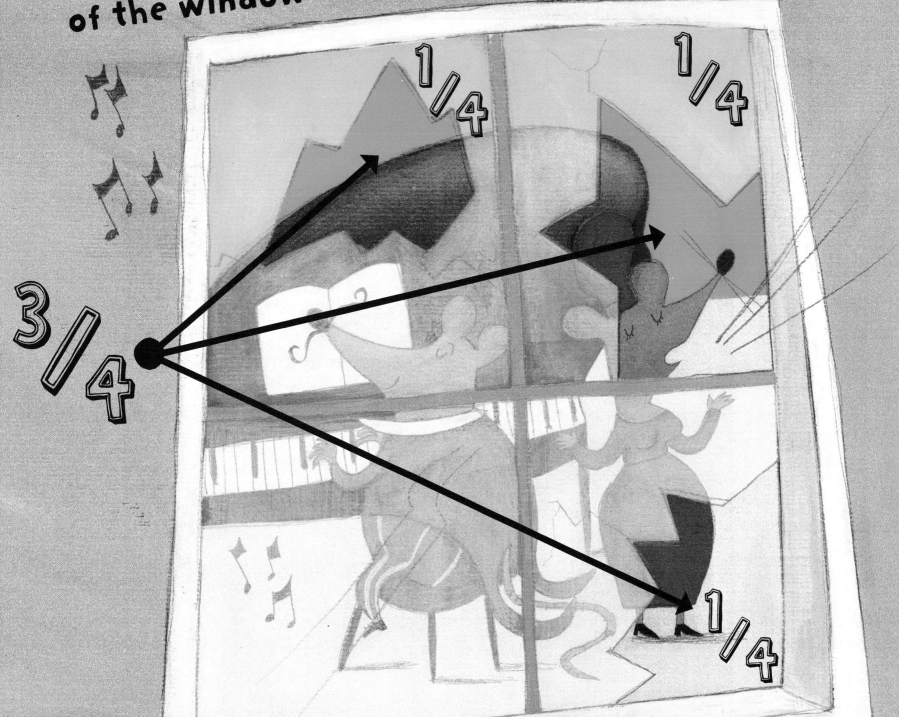

If you were a fraction, you could be divided into eight equal parts. You would be eighths.

Robin slices a raspberry pie into eight pieces. Each bird gets one piece. Each bird gets one-eighth of the pie.

15

If you were a fraction, you could be divided more than once.
You would be one unit subdivided into equal parts.

Josie and Jackie split the yummy candy bar. They each have one-half.

Then Johnny and Joey show up. Josie and Jackie split each part again. Now the candy bar is in four pieces.

Josie, Jackie, Johnny, and Joey each have one-fourth of the candy bar.

If you were a fraction, you could be part of a set.
A set is a group that has something in common.

Louis the tiger trainer has a set of three flaming hoops. Fanny the tiger jumps through the first flaming hoop, or one-third of the set.

Fanny jumps through the second flaming hoop. Fanny has now jumped through two-thirds of the set.

Fanny jumps through the third flaming hoop. Now Fanny has jumped through three-thirds of the set, or one whole set.

If you were a fraction, you could be compared with other fractions.

Buck, Buttercup, and Betsy make six cookies.

Buttercup gets one of the six cookies. She has one-sixth of the cookies.

1/6

Betsy gets three of the six cookies. She has three-sixths, or one-half, of the cookies.

3/6 (1/2)

Buck gets two of the six cookies. He has two-sixths, or one-third, of the cookies.

2/6 (1/3)

One-sixth is the smallest of the three fractions. Buttercup has the fewest cookies. Three-sixths is the largest of the three fractions. Betsy has the most cookies.

You would always be part of the whole ...

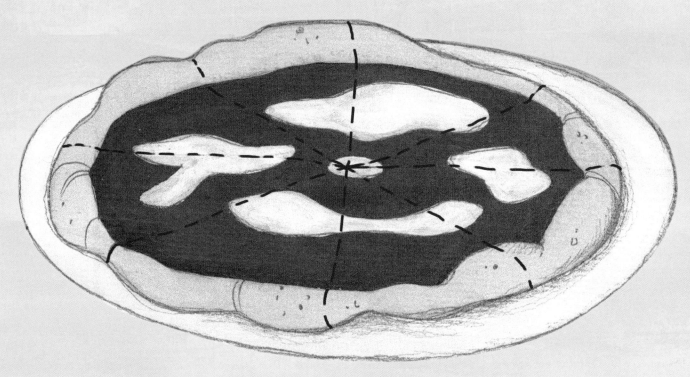

... if you were a fraction.

FRACTION FUN: Make your own pizza pie!

What you need:

- a circular object to trace, such as a coffee can, a Frisbee, or the plastic top from an oatmeal container
- a piece of paper
- scissors
- crayons or markers
- a pencil

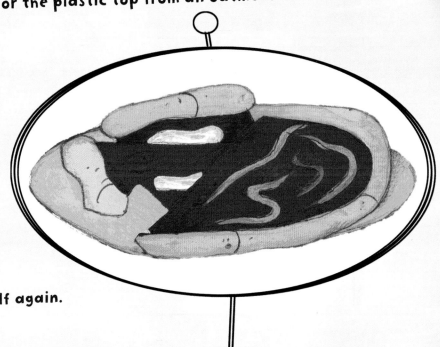

What you do:

1. Trace a circle onto a piece of paper.

2. Cut out the circle.

3. Fold the circle in half. Fold it in half again. Fold it in half again.
   (It will be the shape of an ice-cream cone.)

4. Unfold the paper. Use a pencil to trace the lines where the paper was folded.
   Your lines should create eight equal parts.

5. Use your crayons or markers to draw pizza toppings. You can draw whatever you want on each slice. Here are some ideas: pepperoni, mushrooms, pineapple, sausage, and green peppers. You may want to cover more than one slice with the same topping. You may want to put two toppings on one slice.

6. Now find some fractions in your pizza. If two slices have mushrooms and sausages on them, mushrooms and sausages cover 2/8 (or 1/4) of the pie. If three slices have green peppers on them, green peppers cover 3/8 of the pie. Make a list of the fractions you used.

Glossary

divided—separated into parts or groups

fraction—one or more equal parts of a whole

set—a group that has something in common

subdivided—one thing divided more than once

To Learn More

More Books to Read

Jaffe, Elizabeth Dana. *Can You Eat a Fraction?*
Mankato, Minn.: Yellow Umbrella Books, 2002.

Napoli, Donna Jo. *The Wishing Club: A Story About Fractions.* New York: Henry Holt, 2007.

Pallotta, Jerry. *Apple Fractions.* New York:
Scholastic, 2002.

On the Web

FactHound offers a safe, fun way to find Web sites related to topics in this book. All of the sites on FactHound have been researched by our staff.

1. Visit *www.facthound.com*

2. Type in this special code: 1404847901

3. Click on the FETCH IT button.

Your trusty FactHound will fetch the best sites for you!

Index

Look for all of the books in the Math Fun series:

If You Were a Fraction

If You Were a Minus Sign

If You Were a Plus Sign

If You Were a Set

If You Were an Even Number

If You Were an Odd Number